Guidance

How to use this

This workbook contains over 100 questions specifically designed your child's place value knowledge.
Our years of experience have enabled us to put together the perfect balance of fluency, reasoning questions and vocabulary checks.

Each page is dedicated to one of the current curriculum objectives.

You will find one or two pages of fluency questions. These questions help develop number sense and you will see various questions framed in different ways in order for your child to secure their understanding of the objective.
This means your child will not just be memorising facts, but have a real conceptual understanding.

There will then be a page of reasoning questions.
Reasoning will allow your child to explore these objectives at a deeper level and show if your child has truly mastered these concepts.
It requires children to use mathematical vocabulary, explore trial and error and explain how they have reached their answers.

There will be a space for your child to write their answers down.
If your child prefers to explain this verbally, this is equally acceptable.

After each page is completed, your child can colour in the stars at the top of the page to show how many were correct and they can also use the section on page 28 to colour in. This is a great assessment tool to check the progress and identify any gaps in their knowledge.

For more worksheets and advice- please visit our ever growing and popular website:

www.masterthecurriculum.co.uk

These workbooks are dedicated to Tia, Leanna and Malachi.

MTC Publications

Contents

My Place Value Vocabulary

Place Value

The value of a digit, depending on its position.

For example- the numbers 1,000, 213 and 31 all have the number 1 in it but the place value of 1 is different in all of them.

213 → hundreds, tens, ones

31 → tens, ones

Digit

Any of the ten numbers:
0, 1, 2, 3 ,4, 5, 6, 7 ,8 ,9

The number 552 has three digits.

Hundreds, Tens and Ones

A three-digit number has hundreds, tens and ones.

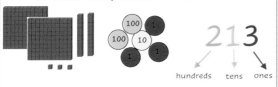

213 → hundreds, tens, ones

Hundreds	Tens	Ones
2	1	3

Thousands

A four-digit number has Thousands, hundreds, tens and ones.

You will work with numbers up to 1,000 in this book.

Thousands	Hundreds	Tens	Ones
●			
1	0	0	0

Numeral

A numeral is a **symbol or name** that stands for a number.

For example: 76, ten, 15 and five hundred are all numerals.

Multiples

A number that can be divided by another number without a remainder.

Multiples of 4:

4   8   12   16   20   24

They are the numbers in the 4 times tables.

My Place Value Vocabulary

Less / Fewer / Fewest

A smaller quantity or amount.

More / Greater / Greatest

A larger quantity or amount.

Compare

Looking at the difference between numbers.

Is one greater than the other?

Are they equal to each other?

6

3

Representation

Pictorial representation - we can use pictures in maths to stand for a number.

These pictures all represent the number 121.

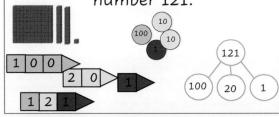

Inequality Symbols

We can use these symbols to tell us if a number is greater than or less than another number.

less than	equal	greater than
<	=	>

204 < 220　　**2 tens = 20**　　**15 > 0**

Partition

To split / separate / divide numbers into smaller parts. This can make calculations easier.

525
↓ ↓ ↓
hundreds tens ones
　5　　　2　　　5

3
↙　↘
2　+　1

My Place Value Vocabulary

Part-Whole Model

A model that shows parts of a number and the whole number.

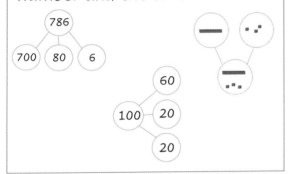

Equal

=

The same amount.

 = 4

The children have an **equal** amount of apples.

Before

146, 147, 148, 149

The number <u>before</u> 147 is 146.

What number comes **before** 100?

95, 96, 97, 98, 99, 100

After

146, 147, 148, 149

The number <u>after</u> 147 is 148.

What number comes **after** 999?

995, 996, 997, 998, 999, 1,000

Next

Similar to the word after.

200, 201, 202, 203...

What comes **next?**

The number 204 is **next**.
200, 201, 202, 203, **204**

Between

The numbers between 200 and 205 are 201, 202, 203 and 204.

200, 201, 202, 203, 2o4, 205

The number between 402 and 404 is 403.

401, 402, 403, 404, 405, 406

My Place Value Vocabulary

Place Value Counters

Counters that can help you find the hundreds, tens and ones in a number.

245 has 2 hundreds, 4 tens and 5 ones.

Place Value Chart

A chart or grid to show the place value of the digits in a number.

Hundreds	Tens	Ones
2	1	3

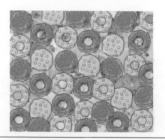

Base 10

Equipment to help you see the thousands, hundreds, tens and ones in a number.

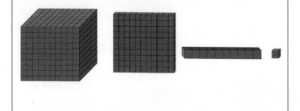

Estimate

A reasonable guess.

Estimate the number of doughnuts.

Strategy

A plan to help you get the answer.

There are many strategies you can use in maths.

Partitioning

525

hundreds tens ones
5   2   5

22 24 ? 28

Number lines

+ 10   + 1

Drawing a picture

Using your fingers

Using equipment

6 0

1

My Place Value Vocabulary

Sequence

A sequence is a list of numbers, shapes or objects in an order. Sequences do not have to have a pattern, but they normally do.

2, 4, 6, 8, ...

3 sides   4 sides   5 sides   6 sides

First, I brush my teeth. Next, I have breakfast. Then I get dressed.

Pattern

Like a sequence. It is a list of numbers, shapes or objects in an order, but it follows a rule and is repeated.

2, 4, 6, 8, ...

Even Numbers

Even numbers can be shared equally when they are whole. You can spot even numbers visually.
Even numbers end in 0,2,4,6 and 8.

Odd Numbers

Odd numbers can not be shared equally when they are whole. You can spot odd numbers visually.
Odd numbers end in 1,3,5,7 and 9.

  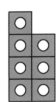 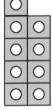

Ascending

From smallest to greatest.
Ascend means 'up'.

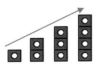

| 45 | 132 | 474 | 499 | 700 |

The number cards have been ordered in **ascending** order.

Descending

From greatest to smallest.
Descend means 'down'.

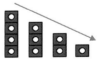

| 700 | 499 | 474 | 132 | 45 |

The number cards have been ordered in **descending** order.

Lesson 1
Count from 0 in multiples of 4

Use this 100 square grid to practise counting in fours.

What do you notice about all of your numbers?

They are all even.
This means that they always end in 0, 2, 4, 6 or 8.

When you feel confident, practise your skill on pages 14-15.

1	2	3	4	5	6	7	8	9	10
11	12	13	14	15	16	17	18	19	20
21	22	23	24	25	26	27	28	29	30
31	32	33	34	35	36	37	38	39	40
41	42	43	44	45	46	47	48	49	50
51	52	53	54	55	56	57	58	59	60
61	62	63	64	65	66	67	68	69	70
71	72	73	74	75	76	77	78	79	80
81	82	83	84	85	86	87	88	89	90
91	92	93	94	95	96	97	98	99	100

Practise counting in fours until you do not need this 100 square grid.
Can you start with any multiple of four?

Lesson 2
Count from 0 in multiples of 8

Use this 100 square grid to practise counting in eights.

Do you notice that counting in fours is similar to counting in eights?

When you feel confident, practise your skill on pages 16-17.

1	2	3	4	5	6	7	8	9	10
11	12	13	14	15	16	17	18	19	20
21	22	23	24	25	26	27	28	29	30
31	32	33	34	35	36	37	38	39	40
41	42	43	44	45	46	47	48	49	50
51	52	53	54	55	56	57	58	59	60
61	62	63	64	65	66	67	68	69	70
71	72	73	74	75	76	77	78	79	80
81	82	83	84	85	86	87	88	89	90
91	92	93	94	95	96	97	98	99	100

Practise counting in eights until you do not need this 100 square grid.
Can you start with any multiple of eight?

Lesson 3
Count from 0 in multiples of 50

Do you notice that counting in 5s is similar to counting in 50s?

What do you notice about all of your numbers?

They all end in 0.

When you feel confident, practise your skill on pages 18-19.

10	20	30	40	50	60	70	80	90	100
110	120	130	140	150	160	170	180	190	200
210	220	230	240	250	260	270	280	290	300
310	320	330	340	350	360	370	380	390	400
410	420	430	440	450	460	470	480	490	500
510	520	530	540	550	560	570	580	590	600
610	620	630	640	650	660	670	680	690	700
710	720	730	740	750	760	770	780	790	800
810	820	830	840	850	860	870	880	890	900
910	920	930	940	950	960	970	980	990	1,000

Practise counting in multiples of 50 until you do not need this grid.
Can you start with any multiple of fifty?

Lesson 4
Count from 0 in multiples of 100

Do you notice that counting in 1s and 10s is similar to counting in 100s?

What do you notice about all of your numbers?

They all end in 0.

When you feel confident, practise your skill on pages 20-21.

10	20	30	40	50	60	70	80	90	100
110	120	130	140	150	160	170	180	190	200
210	220	230	240	250	260	270	280	290	300
310	320	330	340	350	360	370	380	390	400
410	420	430	440	450	460	470	480	490	500
510	520	530	540	550	560	570	580	590	600
610	620	630	640	650	660	670	680	690	700
710	720	730	740	750	760	770	780	790	800
810	820	830	840	850	860	870	880	890	900
910	920	930	940	950	960	970	980	990	1,000

Practise counting in multiples of 100 until you do not need this grid.
Can you start with any multiple of 100?

Lesson 5
Recognise the place value of each digit in a 3-digit number

When you see a three-digit number, you will need to understand what each digit represents.

Hundreds Tens Ones

These images help you understand this.

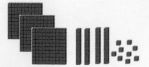

Hundreds	Tens	Ones
3	4	9

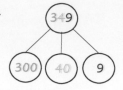

If I had 5 hundreds, 4 ones and 6 tens, what number would this be?
Some might say 546 but it is 564.
When you read the question properly, you can see it has 5 hundreds, 4 ones and 6 tens.

When you feel confident, practise your skill on pages 28-29.

This is the number 564.

Lesson 6
Identify, represent and estimate numbers

As you learnt in the vocabulary section, numbers can be represented in different ways.

Look at all of the ways these numbers have been represented.

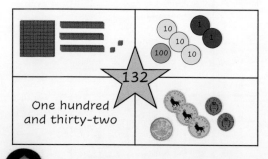

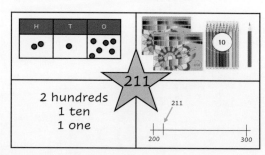

When you feel confident, practise your skill on pages 30-33.

Can you use equipment or drawings to represent the number 700, 319 and 48?

Lesson 7
Find 10 more or less than a given number

When we find 10 more or less than a given number within 1,000 you will need to look at your tens digits and your hundreds digit.

Some numbers are easier than others to find 10 more or 10 less.

For example, 10 more than 547 involves adding 1 ten to the tens column. This becomes 557.

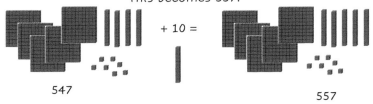

10 less than 547 involves taking 1 ten from the tens column. This becomes 537.

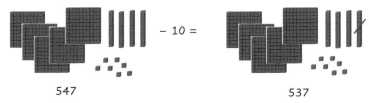

Some numbers are a bit trickier because the tens digit will change and also the hundreds digit will change.

For example, 10 more than 294.　　　When I add 10 more, I have 10 tens.

10 tens makes 100.

This is my 10 tens!

I now have 304.

Let's look at 10 less than 406.

There are no tens. We can make 10s by exchanging the 100 for 10 tens.

Now, we can take 1 ten.

This becomes 396.

When you feel confident, practise your skill on pages 22-24.

Finding 100 more than a number.

When we add 100 to a number, the hundreds column changes,
unless your hundred is a 9. It increases by 1. Let's look at some examples.

116 has 1 hundred.

When I add another 100, it becomes
216 because it has 2 hundreds.

900 has 9 hundreds.

When I add another 100, it becomes
10 hundreds. We say 1,000 because
10 hundreds is equal to 1,000

83 has 0 hundreds.

When I add 100, it becomes 183.

Finding 100 less than a number.

When we take away 100 from a number, the hundreds column changes,
unless your hundred is a 0 in some cases. The hundreds decrease by 1.
Let's look at some examples.

325 has 3 hundreds.

When I subtract 1 hundred, it becomes
225 because it now has 2 hundreds.

1,000 has 0 hundreds.

When you feel
confident, practise
your skill on pages
25-27.

Remember! 1,000 is the same as
10 hundreds. I have exchanged
my thousand for 10 hundreds.

When I subtract 1
hundred, it becomes
9 hundred.

You'll need to remember what these inequality symbols mean.

> This sign means **more than**.
Use this image to help you remember this.

5 is more than 1

< this sign means **less than**.
Use this image to help you remember this.

2 is less than 4

= this sign means equal to.
Use this image to help you remember this.

2 is equal to 2

Read the statements below so you can understand how they work.

800 > 100

800 is more than 100

708 < 807

708 is less than 807

208 > 131

208 is more than 131

99 < 1,000

99 is less than 1,000

1 < 1,000

1 is less than 1,000

When you feel confident, practise your skill on pages 34–35.

Can you pick two 3-digit numbers and add the inequality symbols? Swap the numbers around. What do you have to do with the inequality symbols? They will also have to change!

You will have to order numbers up to 1,000.

You might be asked to order numbers in **ascending** order
(from smallest to biggest)
or **descending** order (biggest to smallest.)

| 506 | 741 | 782 | 817 |

Ascending Order

Smallest to Biggest

| 439 | 325 | 318 | 6 |

Descending Order

Biggest to Smallest

When looking at your numbers, ask yourself, does it have
one, two or three digits?

One-digit numbers are always smaller than two and three-digit numbers and
two-digit numbers are smaller than three-digit numbers.

Sometimes, you are given numbers that look similar to each other like these:

247   742   217   244   724

Step 1: Check your hundreds digits. The number/s with the lowest hundred
digit will be part of the smallest numbers.

What happens if you have numbers with the same hundreds digit?

247   217   244

Step 2: Check your tens digits. The one with the lowest tens digit will be part
of the smallest numbers.

247   217   244

Step 3: If you still have a number with the same hundreds and tens digit, then
check your ones digits. The one with the lowest ones digit will be the
smallest.

When you feel
confident, practise
your skill on pages
36-37.

247   244 ← Smallest!

Roll a dice and make some 3-digit numbers.
Can you order them from smallest to biggest and biggest to smallest?

Lesson 11
Read and write numbers to at least 1,000 in numerals and words

Do you know how to read and write all of the numbers to 1,000?

When looking at a number in digits, read it from left to right.

405 – This number has 4 hundreds so I say four hundred.
It has zero tens so I do not say any tens. It has 5 ones.
So I say **four hundred and five**.

862 – This number has 8 hundreds so I say eight hundred.
It has 6 tens so I say sixty. It has 2 ones. So I say **eight hundred and sixty-two**.

Use the list below to help you write the numbers you find tricky.

1	2	3	4	5	6	7	8	9	10
one	two	three	four	five	six	seven	eight	nine	ten

11	12	13	14	15	16	17	18	19	20
eleven	twelve	thirteen	fourteen	fifteen	sixteen	seventeen	eighteen	nineteen	twenty

20	30	40	50	60	70	80	90	100
twenty	thirty	forty	fifty	sixty	seventy	eighty	ninety	One hundred

100	200	300	400	500	600	700	800	900	1,000
one hundred	two hundred	three hundred	four hundred	five hundred	six hundred	seven hundred	eight hundred	nine hundred	One thousand

When you feel confident, practise your skill on pages 38-39.

Some common mistakes that are made:

The number 40 is written as forty, not fourty.
Eight can be tricky at first.
Ninety still has the e on the end of the word.

Make some 3-digit numbers and practise reading and writing them.

1. Count in steps of 4 from the given number.

12 ➡ ☐ ☐ ☐ ☐

0 ➡ ☐ ☐ ☐ ☐

24 ➡ ☐ ☐ ☐ ☐

2. How many legs can you see? Count in fours.

3. Continue the pattern on the caterpillar.

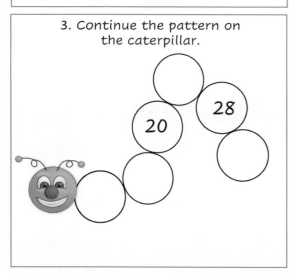

4. How many fingers can you count? Count in fours.

5. Leanna has sixteen football cards. She collects four football cards every day. Use the number track to show how many football cards she will collect after 5 days.

Leanna now has _____ football cards.

6. There are 4 cars in each box. How many cars are there altogether?

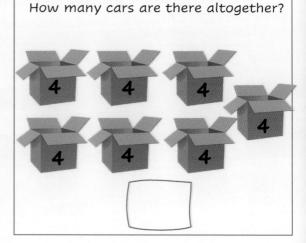

1. Always, Sometimes, Never?

> Multiples of four end in even numbers.

Do you agree?
Explain your answer.

Explain or prove your answers here.

2.

Leanna says:

> The number sequence is in multiples of 4.
> The seventh number will be 152.

| 80 | 84 | 88 | 92 |

Do you agree?
Explain your answer.

Explain or prove your answers here.

3. Spot the odd one out.
Pop it by adding a cross.

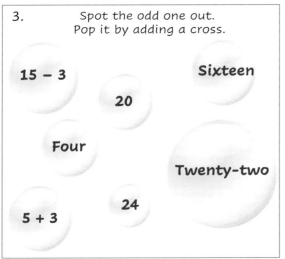

15 – 3   Sixteen
    20
Four
    Twenty-two
    24
5 + 3

Explain or prove your answers here.

1. Count in steps of 8 from the given number.

16 ⇒ ☐ ☐ ☐ ☐

0 ⇒ ☐ ☐ ☐ ☐

48 ⇒ ☐ ☐ ☐ ☐

2. How many legs can you see? Count in eights.

3. Continue the pattern on the caterpillar.

4. How many legs can you count? Count in eights.

5. Tia has twenty-four football cards. She collects eight football cards every day. Use the number track to show how many football cards she will collect after three days.

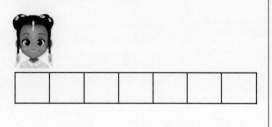

Tia now has _____ football cards.

6. Each pizza has 8 slices. Malachi ordered 5 pizzas.

How many slices are there altogether?

1. Envelopes come in boxes of 8.

I need 6 boxes to have 48 envelopes.

Do you agree?
Explain your answer.

Explain or prove your answers here.

2.

Rosie says:

The number sequence is in multiples of 8.
The seventh number will be 152.

| 104 | 112 | 120 | 128 |

Do you agree?
Explain your answer.

Explain or prove your answers here.

---

3. There are 88 people at a party.
Each pizza is cut into 8 slices.

I ordered 10 boxes of pizza so everyone can have a whole slice.

Is Zach correct?

Explain or prove your answers here.

1. Count in steps of 50 from the given number.

100 ➡ ☐ ☐ ☐

500 ➡ ☐ ☐ ☐

350 ➡ ☐ ☐ ☐

0 ➡ ☐ ☐ ☐

2. How many pounds altogether?

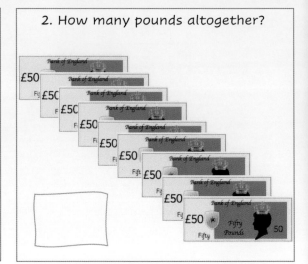

3. Continue the pattern on the caterpillar.

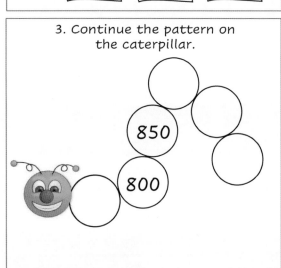

850

800

4. How many sweets are there altogether?

5. What numbers are next in the sequence?

600, 650, 700, _____ , _____

900, 850, 800, _____ , _____

1,000, 950, 900, _____ , _____

250, 200, 150, _____ , _____

6. Pop the multiples of 50 by crossing them out.

500

ten

450

5

605

25

755

15

fifty

35

30

800

1. Always, Sometimes, Never True?

All multiples of 50 end in 0.

Explain or prove your answers here.

---

2. Rosie is learning to count in multiples of 50.

The seventh number in the sequence would be the number 350 if I started from 50.

True or False?
Explain your answer.

Explain or prove your answers here.

3.

What is the same and what is different about counting in 5s and 50s?

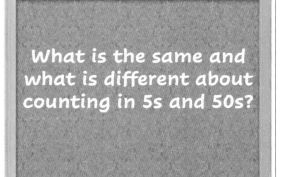

Explain or prove your answers here.

Number and Place Value
Count from 0 in multiples of 100

1. Count in steps of 100 from the given number.

100 ➡ ⬜ ⬜ ⬜

500 ➡ ⬜ ⬜ ⬜

700 ➡ ⬜ ⬜ ⬜

0 ➡ ⬜ ⬜ ⬜

2. There are 100 pencils in each pack of pencils.

I ordered 10 packs!

How many pencils has Zach ordered?

⬜

3. Continue the pattern on the caterpillar.

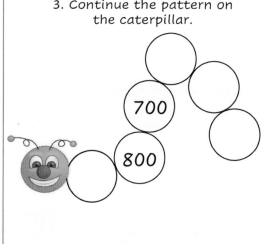

700

800

4. How many sweets are there altogether?

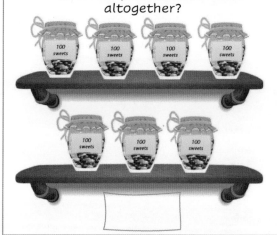

5. What numbers are next in the sequence?

600, 700, 800, _____ , _____

100, 200, 300, _____ , _____

1,000, 900, 800, _____ , _____

800, 700, 600, _____ , _____

6. Pop the multiples of 100 by crossing them out.

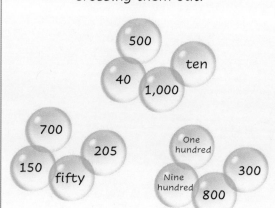

500

ten

40

1,000

700

205

One hundred

150

fifty

Nine hundred

300

800

1.

What is the same and what is different about counting in 1s and 100s?

Explain or prove your answers here.

2. Malachi is learning to count in multiples of 100.

> I count backwards in one hundreds from 800.
>
> The sixth number I say will be 600.

True or False?
Explain your answer.

Explain or prove your answers here.

3. Always, Sometimes, Never True?

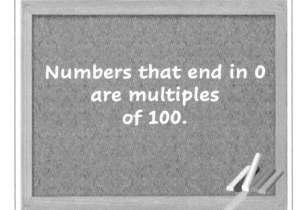

Numbers that end in 0 are multiples of 100.

Explain or prove your answers here.

1. Write the number which is ten more.

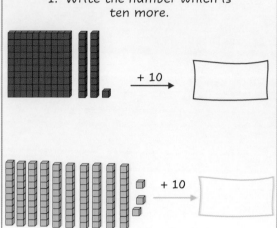

+ 10

+ 10

2. Write the number which is ten less.

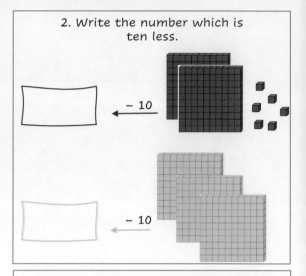

− 10

− 10

3. Complete the table with digits.

10 less	Number	10 more

4. Complete the table with digits.

10 less	Number	10 more

5. Starting with 145, how many tens do you need to add to get more than 200?

Starting with 207, how many tens do you need to add to get more than 300?

6. Count on in tens from 99 to 189. How many tens did you count?

Starting with 66, how many tens do you need to add to get more than 100?

7. Write the number which is ten more.

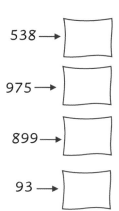

538 →

975 →

899 →

93 →

8. Keep adding 10.

34

658

293

9. Write the answer in the box.

147 + 10 =

347 + 10 =

943 – 10 =

930 – 10 =

10.

What is the number 10 less than 789?

What is the number 10 more than 215?

What is the number 10 less than 603?

11. Ten less than the number is?

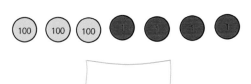

Ten less than the number is?

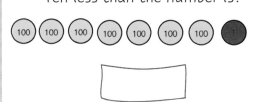

12. Ten less than the number is?

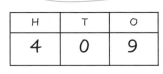

Th	H	T	O
O			

H	T	O
4	0	9

1.

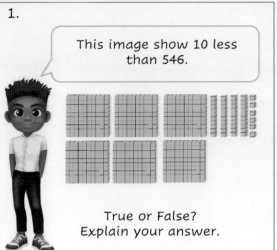

This image show 10 less than 546.

True or False?
Explain your answer.

Explain or prove your answers here.

2.

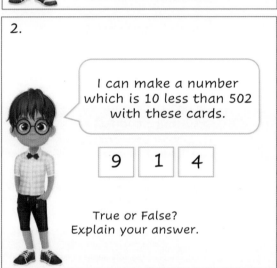

I can make a number which is 10 less than 502 with these cards.

9 1 4

True or False?
Explain your answer.

Explain or prove your answers here.

3.

Leanna says:

When I add 10 to 973, I only change one digit.

Do you agree?
Explain your answer.

Explain or prove your answers here.

1. Write the number which is one hundred more.

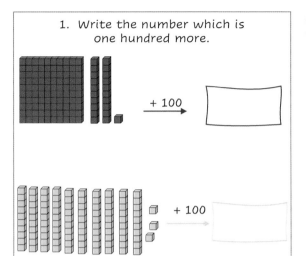

+ 100 →

+ 100 →

2. Write the number which is one hundred less.

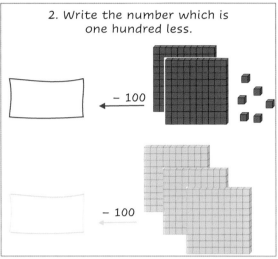

← – 100

← – 100

3. Complete the table with digits.

100 less	Number	100 more

4. Complete the table with digits.

100 less	Number	100 more

5. Starting with 145, how many hundreds do you need to add to get more than 700?

Starting with 207, how many hundreds do you need to add to get more than 300?

6. Count on in hundreds from 89 to 589.
How many hundreds did you count?

Starting with 207, how many hundreds do you need to add to get more than 500?

7. Write the number which is one hundred more.

396 →

180 →

600 →

43 →

8. Keep adding 100.

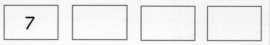
7

294

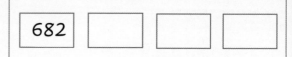
682

9. Write the answer in the box.

457 + 100 =

44 + 100 =

803 − 100 =

1,000 − 100 =

10.

What is the number 100 less than 789?

What is the number 100 more than 215?

What is the number 100 less than 603?

11. One hundred less than the number is?

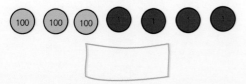

One hundred less than the number is?

12. One hundred more than the number is?

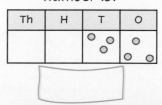

Th	H	T	O

H	T	O
9	0	0

1.

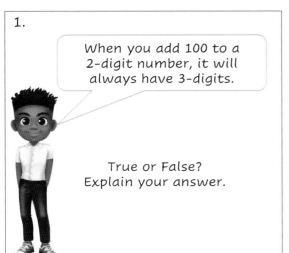

When you add 100 to a 2-digit number, it will always have 3-digits.

True or False?
Explain your answer.

Explain or prove your answers here.

2.

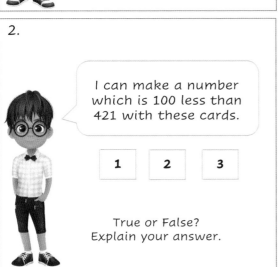

I can make a number which is 100 less than 421 with these cards.

| 1 | 2 | 3 |

True or False?
Explain your answer.

Explain or prove your answers here.

3.

Leanna's sister has 291 marbles.

I have 100 less marbles than my sister. Jar B is mine.

281 marbles   119 marbles   191 marbles

A   B   C

Do you agree?
Explain your answer.

Explain or prove your answers here.

Number and Place Value

Recognise the place value of each digit in a three-digit number (hundreds, tens, ones)

---

1. How many hundreds, tens and ones are there in the following numbers?

463

____ hundreds , ____ tens and ____ ones.

700

____ hundreds , ____ tens and ____ ones.

---

2. Circle the numbers between 700 and 805.

344

804

615

774

45

806

700

805

---

3. Circle the numbers with 4 tens.

474

342

44

174

445

434

140

443

400

---

4. What is the value of the number underlined?

1**7**3 _____

799 _____

37**8** _____

40**1** _____

---

5. What does the number 9 represent in these numbers? ones, tens or hundreds?

379 _____

907 _____

190 _____

92 _____

---

6. Break down these numbers into hundreds, tens and ones.

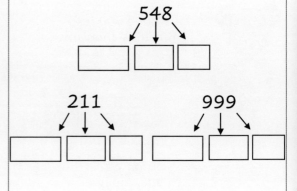

548

211

999

MTC Publications

7. What is the greatest number you can make with the digit cards?

2   6   5

What is the second greatest number you can make?

What is the third smallest number you can make?

8. Match the number sentences to the correct number.

| 634 | 324 | 474 | 194 |

| 300 + 20 + 4 | 200 + 120 + 4 | 100 + 220 + 4 |

Use your place value knowledge!

9. Write a number sentence to show the number partitioned.

367   843   909

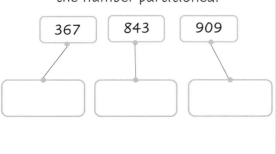

10. How many ways can you partition the following number?

672

11. Fill in the missing numbers.

500 + 20 + 5 = 525

400 + 120 + 5 = 525

300 + 220 + 5 = _____

200 + _____ + 5 = 525

_____ + _____ + 5 = 525

12. Fill in the missing numbers.

800 + 60 + 8 = 868

800 + 50 + 18 = 868

800 + 40 + 28 = _____

800 + 30 + _____ = 868

800 + _____ + _____ = 868

1.

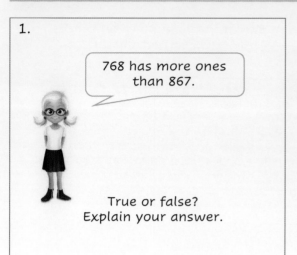

768 has more ones than 867.

True or false?
Explain your answer.

Explain or prove your answers here.

2. What is Malachi's number?

My number has 4 ones, 6 hundreds and 0 tens. What number am I thinking of?

Represent it in a different way.

Explain or prove your answers here.

3. Rosie and Tia partition the number 843.

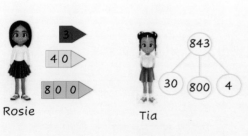

Rosie

Tia

Who is correct?
Explain how you know.

Explain or prove your answers here.

1. Identify the number represented.

Hundreds	Tens	Ones
100 100 100 100 100 100	10 10 10 10 10 10 10 10 10 10 10	● ●

Digits: _____

Word:_____

_____

2. Identify the number represented.

Hundreds	Tens	Ones
■ ■ ■	‖‖‖	▪

Digits: _____

Word:_____

_____

3. Represent the number **583** as a part-whole model.

4. Represent the number **673** as a drawing.

5. Circle the letter which is closest to **600**.

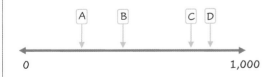

```
        A     B        C D
        ↓     ↓        ↓ ↓
◄───────────────────────────►
0                        1,000
```

Circle the letter which is closest to **540**.

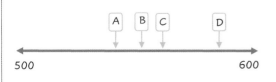

```
              A   B C      D
              ↓   ↓ ↓      ↓
◄───────────────────────────►
500                        600
```

6. Estimate where the number 100 would go on the number lines.

```
|                              |
0                          1,000
```

```
|                              |
0                            200
```

```
|                              |
0                            500
```

7. Identify the number represented.

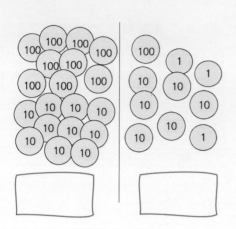

8. How many books are there altogether?

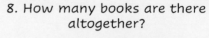

9. What number?

1000s	100s	10s	1s

10. What number?

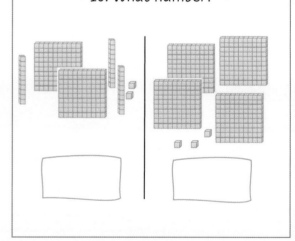

11. Draw an arrow to show where the number would go.

245

| | | | | | | | | | |
200   300

800

| | | | |
0   1,000

12. Draw a number line from 0 – 500.

Mark the following numbers:

49, 400, 320

1. Malachi wants to buy a book with a price of 31p. He has three 10p coins and fifty 1p coins. How many different ways can he make to buy this book?

Explain or prove your answers here.

2. Which of the following is different from the others?

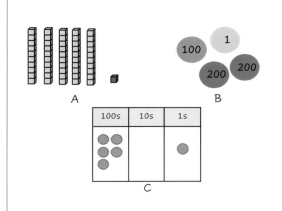

Explain or prove your answers here.

3. Here is a number line and the number 340 on it.

What could the start and end numbers be?

Find three possible solutions. Explain your reasoning.

Explain or prove your answers here.

1. Use inequality symbols to make this correct.

> = <

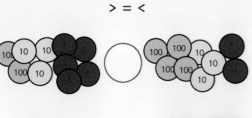

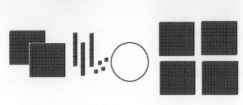

2. Use inequality symbols to make this correct.

> = <

630 ◯ 636

6 hundreds, 8 tens and 7 ones ◯ 687

100 ◯ ten tens

3. Use inequality symbols.

> = <

4. Fill in a number to make this true. Use hundreds, tens and ones.

100 + ____ + 5 > 100 + 60 + 5

____ + 80 + 1 > 800 + 80 + 1

400 + 80 + ____ < 400 + 80 + 7

5. Add the words **greater** or **less** to make the statement correct.

653 is _____than 289

109 is _____than 901

642 is _____than 659

381 is _____than 318

6. Use the signs below to make these true.

> = <

H	T	O
7	8	4

◯

H	T	O
7	4	8

H	T	O
2	1	6

◯

H	T	O
2	6	1

7. Circle the smallest number in each row.

| 355 | 957 | 133 | 683 |

| 100 | 85 | 535 | 634 |

| 340 | 403 | 204 | 263 |

8. Circle the largest number in each row.

| 146 | 823 | 395 | 414 |

| 1,000 | 556 | 269 | 570 |

| 288 | 982 | 818 | 222 |

9. Use the signs below to make this true.

> = <

301 ☐ 640   649 ☐ 694

980 ☐ 909   762 ☐ 726

492 ☐ 421   301 ☐ 310

10. Use the signs > < = to make this true.

564 ☐ 465   132 ☐ 123

974 ☐ 947   235 ☐ 532

650 ☐ 605   838 ☐ 388

11. Use the signs below to make this true.

> = <

5 hundreds
4 tens and 2 ones ☐ 524

3 hundreds
2 tens and 4 ones ☐ 3 hundreds
2 ones and 4 tens

616 ☐ 6 hundreds
6 tens and 1 one

12. Use the signs below to make this true.

> = <

10 hundreds ☐ 999

767 ☐ 7 hundreds
7 tens and 6 ones

3 hundreds
10 tens and 2 ones ☐ 402

1. Write these numbers in order from the smallest to the largest.

463   634   643   446

[ ] [ ] [ ] [ ]

2. Write these numbers in order from the largest to the smallest.

171   717   711   117

3. Label the numbers 1 – 5.
1 being the smallest.

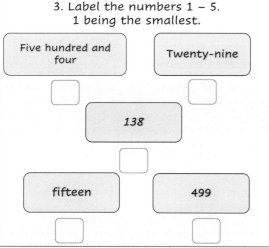

Five hundred and four

Twenty-nine

138

fifteen

499

4. Label the numbers 1 – 5.
1 being the **largest**.

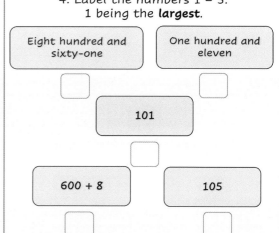

Eight hundred and sixty-one

One hundred and eleven

101

600 + 8

105

5. Label the vintage teddies in order of price from the highest to the lowest.

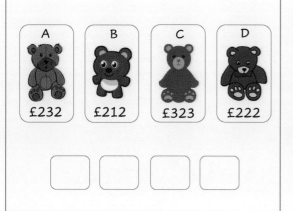

A   B   C   D

£232   £212   £323   £222

[ ] [ ] [ ] [ ]

6. The children took part in a marathon! Order them from last to first.

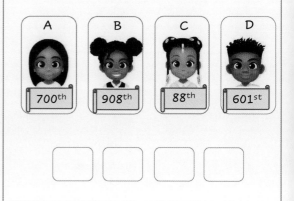

A   B   C   D

700th   908th   88th   601st

[ ] [ ] [ ] [ ]

1. Six friends write a number in their notebooks. Give the answer to the questions below.

613	208	317	620	565	432
Malachi	Tia	Zach	Leanna	Esin	Rosie

A- Who has the smallest number?

B- Who has the second largest number?

C- Who has the number between 320 and 560?

Explain or prove your answers here.

2. Make different 3-digit numbers using the digits 5, 7 and 8. How many numbers can you make? Which number is the **largest**?

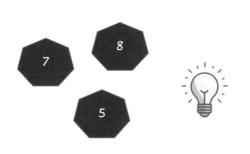

Explain or prove your answers here.

3. Below are 5 numbers:

712	702	655	765	657

Which number is the **furthest** from 700?

How do you know? Explain.

Explain or prove your answers here.

---

1. What number is represented by the picture?

Write it in digits and words.

Digits: _____

Word:_____

_____

---

2. Which number shows five hundred and ninety-six? Pop the bubble by putting a cross.

565   590

519

569   596

---

3. Write the numbers in digits.

four hundred and sixty-seven

two hundred and ninety-two

one hundred and forty-eight

fifty-nine

eight hundred and fifty-five

---

4. Write the numbers in words.

824

908

119

643

---

5. What number is represented by the picture?

Write it in digits and words.

9 0 0

4

Digits: _____

Word:_____

_____

---

6. Draw a line to match the number to the word.

617   670   671

six hundred and seventy-one

six hundred and seventy

six hundred and seventeen

38

MTC Publications

1. Three numbers have been written on a board.

Which one is the odd one out?
Explain your answer.

Explain or prove your answers here.

2. What is the same and what is different about the numbers below?

879   897   987   978

Write the numbers in words when you explain your answer.

Explain or prove your answers here.

3. Spot the mistake.
Explain your answer.

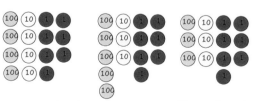

Four hundred and forty-seven.   Five hundred and thirty-seven.   Three hundred and forty-seven.

Explain or prove your answers here.

1. Which alien holds the box that will balance the scales? Circle it.

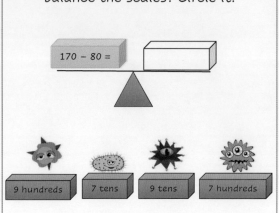

170 – 80 =

| 9 hundreds | 7 tens | 9 tens | 7 hundreds |

2. I caught 200 pokemon.
I wanted to catch 450.
How many more do I need to catch?

3. I have 26 marbles in one jar.
How many marbles do I have to put in the other jar to make 326 altogether?

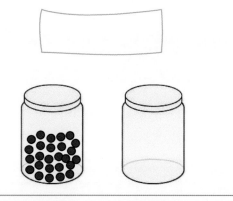

4. The numbers in the triangle add up to 790. Write the missing number.

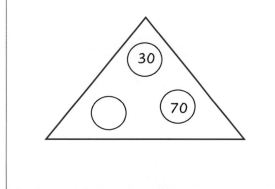

30

70

5. Write the number of eggs on the basket Farmer Joan needs to get 700 altogether.

100 100
100 100

6. Is this correct? If not, what can you do so that it is correct?

Yes ☐   No ☐

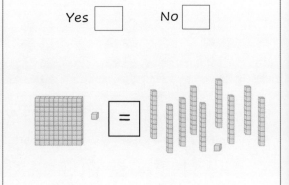

Number and Place Value

Colour in the amount of stars you got correct for each section.

Objective	Fluency	Reasoning
Count from 0 in multiples of 4	☆☆☆☆☆☆	☆☆☆
Count from 0 in multiples of 8	☆☆☆☆☆☆	☆☆☆
Count from 0 in multiples of 50	☆☆☆☆☆☆	☆☆☆
Count from 0 in multiples of 100	☆☆☆☆☆☆	☆☆☆
Find 10 more or less than a given number	☆☆☆☆☆☆ ☆☆☆☆☆☆	☆☆☆
Find 100 more or less than a given number	☆☆☆☆☆☆ ☆☆☆☆☆☆	☆☆☆
Recognise the place value in a three-digit number (hundreds, tens and ones)	☆☆☆☆☆☆ ☆☆☆☆☆☆	☆☆☆
Identify, represent and estimate numbers using different representations	☆☆☆☆☆☆ ☆☆☆☆☆☆	☆☆☆
Compare numbers from 0 up to 1,000	☆☆☆☆☆☆ ☆☆☆☆☆☆	☆☆☆
Order numbers from 0 up to 1,000	☆☆☆☆☆☆ ☆☆☆☆☆☆	
Read and write numbers up to 1,000 in numerals and words	☆☆☆☆☆☆	☆☆☆
Solve number problems and practical problems	☆☆☆☆☆☆	☆☆☆

Turn the page to tick the vocabulary that you know.

MTC Publications

Number and Place Value
Tick the words you know.

Do you know what these words mean? Tick the words that you know.
Go back to the beginning to revise the words you do not know.

Place Value	
Digit	
Hundreds, Tens and Ones	
Thousands	
Numeral	
Multiples	

Less/Fewer /Fewest	
More/Greater/Greatest	
Compare	
Representation	
Inequality Symbols	
Partition	

Part-whole model	
Equal	
Before	
After	
Next	
Between	

Part-whole model	
Equal	
Before	
After	
Next	
Between	

Place Value Counters	
Place Value Chart	
Base 10	
Estimate	
Strategy	

Sequence	
Pattern	
Even Numbers	
Odd Numbers	
Ascending	
Descending	

Answers

Count from 0 in multiples of 4

1. 16, 20, 24, 28.   4, 8, 12, 16.   28, 32, 36, 40
2. 36
3. 12,16,20,24,28,32
4. 24
5. 36 cards.
6. 28 cars.

Reasoning

1. True. Children can write out a sequence to prove this.
2. False. Children should understand that if they are looking for the seventh number- this is 3 more sets of 4, which is 12. Adding 12 more to 92 will not reach 154. The seventh number will be 104.
3. Possible answer: The odd one out is twenty-two. This number is not a multiple of four.

Count from 0 in multiples of 8

1. 24, 32, 40, 48.   8, 16, 24, 32.   56, 64, 72, 80
2. 48
3. 32, 40, 48, 56, 64, 72
4. 64
5. 48 cards.
6. 40 slices.

Reasoning

1. I agree. If I count in eights 6 times, it will equal 48.
2. Rosie is correct. 104, 112, 120, 128, 136, 144, 152. The seventh number is 152.
3. Zach is incorrect. If you count in eights 10 times, you will get the number 80. There will be only 80 slices. He needs another box.

Count from 0 in multiples of 50

1. 150, 200, 250. 500, 550, 600. 400, 450, 500. 50, 100, 150
2. £450
3. 750, 800, 850, 900, 950, 1,000
4. 350 sweets
5. 750, 800.   750, 700.   850, 800.   100, 50
6. 500, 450, fifty, 800

Reasoning

1. Always. If you write a sequence- 0, 50, 100, 150, 200 etc. You can see that they always end in 0.
2. True. Rosie is correct. 50, 100, 150, 200, 250, 300, 350
3. Possible answer: Same: The numbers have the same pattern. Different: 50s have a 0 at the end, whereas 5s sometimes end in a 5.

Count from 0 in multiples of 100

1. 200, 300, 400. 600, 700, 800. , 800, 900, 1,000 100, 200, 300
2. 1,000 pencils.
3. 900, 800, 700, 600, 500, 400
4. 700 sweets.
5. 900, 1,000.   400, 500.   700, 600.   500, 400
6. 500, 1,000, 700, one hundred, nine hundred, 800, 300

Reasoning

1. Same: The first digit always goes up by 1. Different: 100s always end in 0. 100s increase in size by 100 times each time and ones increase by 1 each time.
2. False: 800, 700, 600, 500, 400, 300. The 6ᵗʰ number he says is 300.
3. Sometimes True. 10, 20, 50 are not multiples of 100 but end in 0. 100, 200, 300 are multiples of 100.

Find 10 more or less than a given number

1. 131.   113
2. 196. 290
3. 324, 334, 344.   591, 601, 611.   182, 192, 202
4. 211, 221, 231   384, 394, 404.   380, 390, 400
5. 6.   10
6. 8. 4
7. 548, 985, 909, 103
8. 44, 54, 64. 668, 678, 688. 303, 313, 323
9. 157   357. 933.   920
10. 779,   225,   593
11. 294. 691
12. 990. 399

Reasoning

1. False. It shows 100 more than 546 – 646.
2. False. 10 less than 502 is 492. There isn't a 2 to make this number.
3. I agree in this case. Only the tens digit changes. 983.

Find 100 more or less than a given number

1. 221. 203
2. 106.   200
3. 434, 334, 534.   501, 601, 701.   292, 192, 392
4. 211, 311, 411   204, 304, 404.   380, 480, 580
5. 6 hundreds, 1 hundred
6. 5 hundreds. 3 hundreds
7. 496. 280. 700   143
8. 107, 207, 307.   394, 494, 594,   782, 882, 982
9. 557, 144, 703, 900
10. 689. 315. 703
11. 204. 900
12. 133. 1,000

Reasoning

1. True, 99 is the greatest 2-digit number. Adding 100 will make 199. 11 is the smallest 2-digit number. Adding 100 makes 111. These numbers have 3-digits.
2. Zach is correct. 100 less than 421 is 321.
3. Leanna is incorrect. Jar C is hers.

Answers

Recognise the place value of each digit in a 3-digit number

1. 4 hundreds, 6 tens and 3 ones. 7 hundreds, 0 tens and 0 ones
2. 804, 774
3. 342, 44, 445, 443, 140
4. 7 tens.   7 hundreds.   8 ones.   1 one
5.

    375 ones   907 hundreds

    190 tens   92 tens

6. 500, 40, 8.   200, 10, 1. 900, 90, 9
7. 652.   625.   526
8.

    634   324   474   194

    300 + 20 + 4   200 + 120 + 4   100 + 220 + 4

    367   843   909

9.

    300 + 60 + 7   800 + 40 + 3   900 + 9

10. Various ways. Examples: 600 + 70 + 2. 500 + 170 + 2. 400 + 270 + 2
11. 300 + 220 + 5 = 525.   200 + 320 = 525   100 + 420 + 5 = 525
12. 800 + 40 + 28 = 868.   800 + 30 + 38 = 868.   800 + 20 + 48 = 868

Reasoning

1. True if you are looking at just the ones place. Children can have a discussion that 867 can be made entirely of ones and would therefore have more than 768.
2. 604
3. Rosie is correct. Tia has partitioned the number into 834 instead of 843.

Identify, represent and estimate numbers using different representations

1. 702 – seven hundred and two
2. 331 – three hundred and thirty-one
3. Part whole model- example:

4. Example:

5. B. A
6.

    0 ──────── 1,000

    0 ──────── 200

    0 ──────── 500

7. 1,000.   163
8. 324
9. 234
10. 232. 403
11.

    200 ──────── 300

    ★

    0 ──────── 1,000

12.

    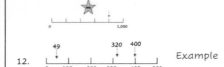

    Example

Reasoning

1. Four ways- thirty-one 1p coins. Twenty-one 1p coins and one 10p coin. Eleven 1p coins and two 10p coins. One 1p coin and three 10p coins.
2. A. It represents the number 51 whilst the others represent the number 501.
3. Start – 0 end – 1,000. start 320, end 380. start 100, end 800. These show sensible intervals between the numbers.

Compare numbers from 0 up to 1,000

1. 235 < 432.   234 < 400
2. 630 < 636.   687 = 687.   100 = 100
3. 300 > 201.   340 > 291
4. 70 – 90   900.   0 – 6
5. greater   less.   less.   greater
6. 784 > 748   216 < 261
7. 133.   85.   204
8. 823.   1,000.   982
9. 301 < 604. 980 > 909.   492 > 421. 649 < 694.   762 > 726. 301 < 310
10. 564 > 465.   974 > 947   650 > 605   132 > 123   235 < 532. 838 > 388
11. 542 > 524.   324 < 342.   616 < 661
12. 1,000 > 999.   767 < 776. 402 = 402

Order numbers from 0 up to 100

1. 446, 463, 634, 643
2. 717, 711, 171, 117
3.

4.

5. C,A,D,B
6. B, A, D, C

Reasoning

Compare and order numbers from 0 up to 100

1. A- 208: Tia   B- 613: Malachi. C- 432: Rosie
2. Six Numbers – 578, 587, 785, 758, 875, 857 Largest: 875
3. 765- It has the most ones away from 700.

Answers

Read and write numbers to at least 1,000

1. Three hundred and ten
2.

565   590

519

569   ✗

3. 467. 292. 148. 59. 855
4. Eight hundred and twenty-four.   Nine hundred and eight.   One hundred and nineteen.   Six hundred and forty-three
5. 904.   Nine hundred and four

6.

617   670   671

six hundred and seventy-one

six hundred and seventy

six hundred and seventeen

Reasoning

1. Fourty because it hasn't been spelt correctly.
2. Various answers. They contain digits 9,8 and 7 but represent different values. Words to be spelt correctly: eight hundred and seventy-nine, eight hundred and ninety-seven, nine hundred and eight, nine hundred and eighty-seven,
3. The last image shows 337, not 347

Solve number problems and practical problems

1.

2. 150
3. 300
4. 690
5. 300
6. No, one more ten needs to be added, or the equals sign needs to be changed to >

Printed in Great Britain
by Amazon

47537720R00027